COLIN A. HOPE

# EGYPTIAN POTTERY

SHIRE EGYPTOLOGY

2

British Library Cataloguing in Publication Data available.

Published by
SHIRE PUBLICATIONS LTD
Cromwell House, Church Street, Princes Risborough,
Aylesbury, Bucks HP17 9AJ, UK

Series Editor: Barbara Adams

ISBN 0 85263 852 3

First published 1987

Set in 11 point Times and printed in Great Britain by
C. I. Thomas & Sons (Haverfordwest) Ltd,
Press Buildings, Merlins Bridge, Haverfordwest, Dyfed.

# Contents

# Acknowledgements

During the course of the preparation of this book I have been assisted greatly by my wife, Nella, who has proofread and typed the original manuscript and commented upon the text; her encouragement has been invaluable. I wish to thank several of my colleagues for placing the result of their research at my disposal (especially Dr Dorothea Arnold, Miss Janine Bourriau and Dr Helen Jacquet-Gordon), and Dr N. Kanawati, Dr B. Ockinga, Mrs Dawn Milne, Mrs Barbara Adams and Ian Edwards for commenting upon preliminary drafts of this book. Johnothan C. Howell prepared many of the figures included here. My gratitude is extended to all of those institutions and their curators who have allowed me to reproduce photographs of pottery in their collections, particularly the Petrie Museum, University College London, in which so many of the objects illustrated are housed.

# List of illustrations

# Chronology

From Murnane, W. J., *The Penguin Guide to Ancient Egypt,* 1983.

| | | |
|---|---|---|
| **Predynastic and Protodynastic** | before 3050 BC | Badarian, Naqada I to III phases |
| **Early Dynastic or Archaic Period** | 3050 to 2686 BC | Dynasties I to II |
| **Old Kingdom** | 2686 to 2181 BC | Dynasties III to VI |
| **First Intermediate Period** | 2181 to 2040 BC | Dynasties VII to XI (Theban) |
| **Middle Kingdom** | 2040 to 1782 BC | Dynasties XI to XII |
| **Second Intermediate Period** | 1782 to 1570 BC | Dynasties XIII to XVII |
| **New Kingdom** | 1570 to 1070 BC | Dynasties XVIII to XX |
| **Third Intermediate Period** | 1070 to 713 BC | Dynasties XXI to XXIV |
| **Late Period** | 713 to 332 BC | Dynasties XXV to XXXI |
| **Graeco-Roman Period** | 332 BC to AD 395 | Ptolemies and Roman Emperors |

**1.** (Above) Drawing of Nubian children burnishing a jar; Deir el-Medina, Nineteenth Dynasty. (After Holthoer, R., *New Kingdom Pharaonic Sites: The Pottery,* figure 26.)

**2.** (Below) Small limestone statuette of a female adding handles (?) to a pot; New Kingdom. (Courtesy of Petrie Museum; UC 15706.)

# 1
# The Egyptian potter

'The potter is under the soil,
Though as yet among the living;
He grubs in the mud more than a pig,
In order to fire his pots.
His clothes are stiff with clay,
His girdle is in shreds;
If air enters his nose,
It comes straight from the fire.
He makes a pounding with his feet,
And is himself crushed;
He grubs the yard of every house
And roams the public places.'

(From 'The Satire of the Trades', Papyrus Sallier II; translation after Lichtheim, M., *Ancient Egyptian Literature I*, 186-7, Berkeley, 1975.)

This quotation from an Egyptian text of Middle Kingdom date shows the Egyptian attitude to the profession of the potter. It was a dirty and uncomfortable occupation and not held in very high esteem. As a craft or profession that of the potter ranked very low on the social scale and potters were amongst the poorer members of Egyptian society, though we know that several did possess land and houses of their own.

The Egyptian word for a potter was *ikd(w)*, which also denoted any builder or fashioner. The term *ikdw n dsw* also occurs, meaning a 'fashioner of *(ds) djes* vessels', and from this the pun *ikd ndst*, a 'fashioner of little' is derived.

The manufacture of pottery in Pharaonic Egypt was a male prerogative, as can be seen from the reliefs of potters at work, and as with many other occupations, skills were passed from father to son. However, most members of a potter's family would have helped out in various ways, for example collecting fuel for the kilns, carrying the clay from its sources or adding the finishing touches to a pot before it was fired. This probably accounts for the rare representation of children or youths burnishing pottery vessels (figure 1). Even rarer is the depiction of women lending a hand, though one small statuette does seem to show a woman perhaps adding handles to a vessel (firgure 2). That women did play a role in pottery making seems possible, especially in the manufacture of handmade pottery, such as dishes for baking bread, though evidence is scant.

The potters produced an enormous quantity of vessels of all shapes and sizes and as their products were necessary in all households and for use in temples and tombs they were an essential element in society. They probably operated in most villages, especially in the larger ones from where their products could have been distributed. They would have been found in greater numbers in the towns and cities. The majority of potters would have used whatever raw clay materials were to hand and made, on demand, a wide range of forms. Where different materials were available some potters may have specialised in using certain types of clay. This was perhaps the case in areas where marl clays as well as the commoner Nile silt clay were found.

In addition to those who provided pottery for the community at large, other potters were employed and worked primarily for the large estates owned by the temples, the wealthy land-owning upper and possibly middle classes and the royal family and the king with his government departments. Their products were included amongst the salaries which were received by people employed by these estates or institutions and which were paid not in money but in food, beer, clothing and the other necesssities of daily life. The specialised communities of artisans who worked on the royal tombs and other state building projects, who were provided with state housing in government-built villages, also received pottery vessels in this way. The potters on such estates worked in conjunction with other craftsmen such as carpenters and metalworkers as well as butchers, bakers and brewers. This can be seen in tomb reliefs as well as from wooden models of craftsmen and others depicting household activities which have been found in tombs.

Whether associated with large estates or working in small villages, the Egyptian potters situated their workshops and kilns on the outskirts of any settlement. Their location would have been determined by access to available clay deposits but also by the need to keep the fumes and smoke from their kilns away from domestic quarters. It is probable that some potters worked on their own while others formed groups which shared one workshop.

Some potters employed by the temples may have specialised in the manufacture of vessels used in the rituals enacted within the temples, such as those for pouring water libations and purification. They may also have supplied similar vessels in the ceremonies connected with burial practices and with offerings made in or at tombs. However, metal vessels were more commonly used for religious purposes. It is probable that certain potters or groups of potters specialised in the manufacture of particular types of pottery. Several clear examples from the New Kingdom exist. During this period some pottery was decorated with elaborate designs in blue, red and black/brown (for example figures 15, 16, 18-20) and its manufacture appears to have been restricted to the principal administrative centres (the sites of Luxor, Amarna and possibly Memphis and Gurob), from where it was distributed. This is indicated by the quantities found at various sites, the standardisation of the decorative scheme used on the various shapes and the use of a rare blue pigment which derives its colour from cobalt. From the first half of the Eighteenth Dynasty date a series of figure vases in the form of women and animals (figure 47). They are comparatively rare, display a high level of technical ability on the part of the potter and are covered with a red polished slip; most were made entirely or partially with a mould. On the other hand, certain aspects of the manufacture of the principal transport and storage jar, the amphora (figure 52), which was not uncommon, indicate a specialisation in its production. These comprise a uniformity of shape, surface treatment and material.

Many vessels preserve a wide variety of marks incised into them, either before or after firing, or painted on them. These are termed potmarks. Some may have indicated the capacity of the vessel, others may have been the personal marks of individual potters, those of workshops, or have indicated ownership (figure 26).

# 2
# Pottery manufacture

## The clays and their preparation

The ancient Egyptian potters had at their disposal two basically different types of clay. The most abundant and frequently used was the alluvial Nile silt clay available throughout Egypt on the banks of the Nile and in the cultivated areas which border the river. It is a very plastic clay, rich in silica and iron oxides, and when fired in an oxidising atmosphere turns a reddish-brown colour. In general the fired body is quite porous and there are often grey cores due to incomplete oxidisation. The second type of clay was the marl clay, which, before treatment, would have been stone-like; it contains a fairly high percentage of calcium carbonates. When fired in an oxidising atmosphere this type of clay will develop a range of colours from pale yellow to green and white. It is found on the desert edge and under the cultivation near the desert, its composition being greatly affected by the nearby limestone; it is of greater geological age than the Nile silt clay. Within each of these two types there are many variations depending upon local conditions in the regions where the clays were formed, and natural mixtures of the two may have occurred. Potters working in the villages and towns may have acquired their clays directly from the local deposits or possibly from farmers on whose land good deposits were to be found. Access to the clay deposits may well have been granted in exchange for pottery vessels. Potters working for private, religious, government or royal estates may have had their clays provided.

The clay was subjected to various processes to make it suitable for the potter. Our source of information on these is the various tomb reliefs. After being dug, the clay might be soaked in a pit with water (levigated), either to break it down and make it workable (particularly necessary in the case of the marls), or to separate the coarser particles, or to mix in any tempering material such as sand, crushed limestone, straw and grog (crushed pottery). Following this it was either kneaded or trodden to produce an even texture and remove excess air (figures 7, 9). The clay was then formed into conical lumps and delivered to the potter (figure 7).

## Manufacturing techniques

Throughout the history of pottery manufacture in Pharaonic

Egypt several different manufacturing techniques were employed. Although it is possible to document a development in these techniques, from vessels entirely handmade to those thrown on a kick-wheel, many of the methods between these two were employed simultaneously and some were retained for certain types or sizes of vessel when they had, in general, been replaced by other, more 'advanced' techniques. The principal methods of manufacture used by the Egyptian potters were: hand-forming, hand-forming and finishing in a stand, and forming on a wheel.

## Hand-forming

This technique was used commonly throughout the Predynastic Period and continued as one of the major forming techniques into the Old Kingdom. Several different hand-forming methods were used. The simplest of these involved fashioning the vessel from a lump of clay with the fingers. Vessels formed in this way were

**3.** Small handmade jar, coarse Nile silt; Abydos, Old Kingdom. (Courtesy of Macquarie University; MU 1990.)

**4.** Hand-modelled
duck vase; black-fired
fine marl clay, bur-
nished, with incised
details; Qurna, Thir-
teenth Dynasty.
(Courtesy of Petrie
Museum; UC 13479.)

necessarily fairly small. A related technique employed the paddle
and anvil, whereby the roughly hand-formed vessel was refined
and its walls thinned by beating with a paddle, supporting the
inner face with an anvil. The anvil was probably a stone and the
paddle a piece of wood. This method was possibly used to
produce thin-walled bowls. The technique of slab building,
although never common, was used particularly in the manufacture of small rectangular or square open-topped 'boxes' or oval
dishes, where the base and sides were formed from separate
hand-formed slabs which were joined.

Another method is that of forming the vessel with the aid of a
mould, which was probably made of baked clay. During the Old
Kingdom some deep, thick-walled bread moulds (figure 27) were
possibly made by pressing clay over a conical mould. Some fine
carinated bowls of the same period (figure 28) may also have
been formed over or in a mould and their shape refined with the
aid of a tool. This technique is very time-consuming and both
types of vessel were also made on a wheel. During the New
Kingdom this method is attested by a series of figure vases
depicting nurses or musicians, all female, and others depicting
animals and birds. They were formed in two or more parts which
were either made separately in moulds or modelled by hand and
then joined. Some of these vessels are amongst the finest pottery
to have survived from ancient Egypt. Similar techniques were
used in the manufacture of human, animal or bird-headed jar lids
(figures 68, 70) from the New Kingdom onwards.

### Hand-forming and finishing in a stand

This technique involved forming the vessel by hand and finishing the neck and rim by standing it in a device which enabled the vessel to be rotated. The bodies of vessels so formed show uneven marks typical of hand-forming while the uppermost parts display roughly parallel marks produced by rotation. The technique, like the wheel itself, may have developed out of the practice of building up a vessel on a mat. It is clearly shown being practised by the standing potters in a relief from the Fifth Dynasty tomb of They at Saqqara (figure 5). The devices in which the jars were placed were small stands, probably of wood or stone, hollowed out and greased to ease rotation. This relief dates many centuries after the date of the development of the technique, which seems to have been during the Naqada II phase of the Predynastic Period, as attested by vessels themselves.

### Forming on a wheel

A logical development from these simple rotating devices was the creation of pivoted wheels which enabled the vessel to be rotated throughout the manufacturing process. Two types of wheel must be distinguished: those which can be rotated at sufficient speed to enable the manipulation of centrifugal force in the manufacturing process (called throwing), and those which are incapable of this. The former is the more advantageous to the potter, enabling him to produce with ease greater numbers of both stronger and more evenly shaped vessels. The latter is more cumbersome and its use restricted; it is often termed a *turntable*.

**5.** Potters, tomb of They; Saqqara, Fifth Dynasty. (After Holthoer, R., *New Kingdom Pharaonic Sites: The Pottery*, figure 4.)

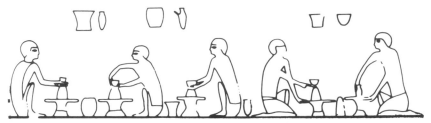

**6.** Potters, tomb of Bakt III; Beni Hasan, Eleventh Dynasty. (After Holthoer, R., *New Kingdom Pharaonic Sites: The Pottery*, figure 14.)

Its existence in Egypt is probably attested by models known from the Old to Middle Kingdoms in which potters are shown working very low wheels with wide wheel-heads. Parts of such wheels have been found dating from the Middle Kingdom to the Third Intermediate Period and they comprise pairs of stones, the upper one of the pair rotating in the lower by means of a mortice and tenon joint. A wooden wheel-head would have been attached to the upper stone, and the lower secured in the ground. Experiments carried out using such a wheel show that small vessels can be formed on them but that they are more suitable for use in applying decoration and finishing the shape of a vessel. The latter is probably depicted in the only relief of a very low wheel, which occurs in the Eighteenth Dynasty tomb of Kenamun at Luxor (figure 12).

Wheels capable of being used for throwing are depicted in reliefs which date from the Fifth Dynasty onwards, the first definite representation occurring in the tomb of They at Saqqara. The first types were low and had detachable wheel-heads which pivoted in a separate axis (figure 5). Middle Kingdom variations on this low wheel possessed pivoted wheel-heads with attached axes, either tall or broad (figures 6, 7), while another type developed with a detached wheel-head which pivoted in a tall axis (figure 8). Several of these types were used during the same

**7.** Pottery workshop, tomb of Amenemhat; Beni Hasan, Twelfth Dynasty. (After Holthoer, R., *New Kingdom Pharaonic Sites: The Pottery*, figure 15.)

**8.** (Left) Potter, tomb of Djehuty-hotep; El-Bersheh, Twelfth Dynasty. (After Holthoer, R., *New Kingdom Pharaonic Sites: The Pottery*, figure 44.)
**9.** (Right) The god Khnum at a kick-wheel; the hieroglyphic caption reads 'Khnum, fashioner of mankind'. The verb 'to fashion' is written with a man using a potter's wheel; El-Hibis, Kharga Oasis, Twenty-Seventh Dynasty. (After Holthoer, R., *New Kingdom Pharaonic Sites: The Pottery*, figure 32.)

period. The tall-axis type was used throughout the New Kingdom and Third Intermediate Period. All of these wheels are depicted being rotated by the potter himself and hence he could not always have used both hands in fashioning the vessel and the speed at which the wheels rotated was not continuous. The achievement of a continuous rotation speed sufficient to enable efficient throwing seems to date from the Twenty-Seventh Dynasty and the introduction of the kick-wheel. This wheel comprises a lower part, the fly-wheel, which is kicked by the potter, rotating an axis to which the wheel-head is attached (figure 9).

Manufacturing techniques employed on the types of wheels described were generally similar but some chronological distinction can be seen in the finishing processes. A vessel could be made from one piece of clay, the part from which it was fashioned being cut by means of a piece of string (figures 6, 7) or built up from sections. Rarely, part of a vessel was formed by hand and attached to the remainder which was wheel-made; this technique was in use until the end of the New Kingdom. Until the Second Intermediate Period a feature of the exterior of most vessels is the roughness of the lower body and base, which show the random marks created when they were scraped once dry. The interiors of these vessels show the continuous internal spiral and rilling marks, stopping below the rim in most cases. From the Second Intermediate Period the technique developed of finishing the base by carefully removing excess clay from the dry pot once it had been inverted upon the wheel head; scraping marks became less common. This does not occur on closed vessels until the end of that period, is rare before the early Eighteenth Dynasty but became standard by the middle of that dynasty. Rilling marks on the interior of the vessel continue without interruption from the base to the rim. With the development of the kick-wheel pottery could be thrown completely on the wheel with greater ease and

**10.** Nile-silt, wheel-made jars with scraping marks; Beni Hasan, late Eleventh to Twelfth Dynasties. (Courtesy of Macquarie University; left to right, MU 1428, 2251.)

**11.** Types of base formation — ring bases: *left,* applied (Middle Kingdom, Esna, MU 1471), *centre left,* thrown (Late Period, MU 1773); round bases: *centre right,* scraped (Middle Kingdom, Beni Hasan, MU 1446), *right,* trimmed (early Eighteenth Dynasty, Esna, MU 1468). (Courtesy of Macquarie University.)

efficiency. In addition to the use of tools in the scraping to shape of the lower body, it is probable that they were also used throughout Dynastic times as an aid in forming the profile and in forming or finishing rims. For the latter, cloths could also have been used.

Before the shape of any vessel could be so refined it was allowed to dry in the open air to what is called the leather-hard stage. Subsequently the surface may have been smoothed by the potter's hands or with a cloth, after which a coating either of a pigment and water (a wash) or pigment, clay and water (a slip) could be added to the surface. Such coatings served to make the surface less permeable, improve the appearance, imitate other materials or provide a suitable surface for painted decoration. This was probably also the purpose of compacting the surface by rubbing it with a pebble (burnishing; figure 1) or a cloth (polishing). The vessel could be decorated by a variety of techniques. When completely dry it was ready for the kiln.

### Kilns

Our knowledge of Egyptian pottery kilns is derived from the few examples which have survived and representations in tomb reliefs, models and hieroglyphic signs. Old Kingdom examples seem to have flared to the top, with straight or concave sides; they were about the height of a man, varied between 1.00 and 3.00 metres (3 feet 3 inches to 9 feet 10 inches) in diameter and, like all kilns from Egypt, were made of mud bricks (figure 5). Vessels were loaded into the kiln from the top and stacked on openwork platforms which separated them from the fire located in a small chamber below. The tops were sealed with a temporary

**12.** (Above) Pottery manufacture, tomb of Kenamun; Qurna, mid Eighteenth Dynasty. (After Holthoer, R., *New Kingdom Pharaonic Sites: The Pottery*, figure 24.)
**13.** (Below) Reconstruction of a kiln; East Karnak, Late Period. (After Redford, D. B., 'Son of Sun-Disc', *Archaeological Newsletter*, Royal Ontario Museum, New Series, number 154, figure 1.)

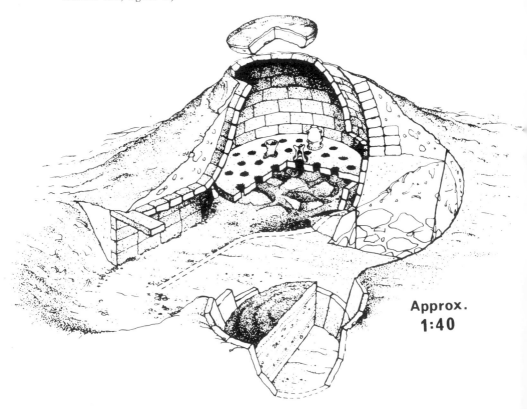

Approx.
**1:40**

structure, probably branches and mud, on each firing; fuel (brushwood and such like) was inserted into the firing chamber through a hole in the lower wall, around which was a projecting wall. This design changed little in succeeding periods. Middle Kingdom kilns seem to have tapered to the top (figure 7) or have been cylindrical, and one extant example was 2.40 metres (7 feet 10 inches) in diameter. This is roughly the same dimension as a New Kingdom kiln found at Luxor; the relief from the tomb of Kenamun indicates that the kiln height had increased by the New Kingdom, its shape flaring to the top with concave sides (figure 12). Later examples show this type and the tapering type to have continued in use (figure 13). These simple up-draught kilns were able to reach temperatures ranging from 600 to 1100 C (1100 to 2000 F), with 600 to 900 C (1100 to 1650 F) sufficient for Nile-silt vessels and 700 to 1100 C (1300 to 2000 F) for marl-clay vessels.

# 3
# Decoration

Throughout the course of dynastic history the Egyptian potters used a wide range of decorative techniques and motifs, certain of which gained greater favour during particular periods. These comprise: application of motifs, burnishing, fenestration (the cutting out of sections of the wall), incision, modelling of the vessel wall and painting. No glazed pottery was produced. Several techniques could be used on the same vessel. In addition to these methods of decoration, the shapes of many vessels, despite any functional considerations, are in themselves decorative and display a desire for balance and symmetry. This is aptly illustrated by a magnificent vessel from the so-called Embalmers' Cache of King Tutankhamun of the Eighteenth Dynasty found in the Valley of the Kings (figure 14). The slender neck and flaring mouth of the vessel derive their shape from that of the blue lotus flower so highly esteemed by the Egyptians. The same flower was the inspiration for the shape of large chalices manufactured during the New Kingdom (figure 66), as was that of the white lotus. Shape and decoration, especially painted motifs, often combined to simulate the prototype.

**Applied decoration**
The technique of applying decorative elements to the exterior of the vessel, always done before it was fired, is known intermittently from the Archaic Period onwards, becoming more common from the Second Intermediate Period. The elements were either fashioned by hand from pieces of clay or formed in moulds. In its simplest form this technique is encountered on vessels of the Middle Kingdom to Second Intermediate Period which have small pieces of clay or miniature vessels attached to their rims or necks, often in combination with incised designs (figure 34). Occurring from this timespan, but also from the New Kingdom, are femino-form jars which have small, often crude, mould-made or finger-modelled faces attached to the rim, and arms on the neck and upper body, with hands sometimes cupping breasts (figure 62). In the New Kingdom this type of decoration was often accompanied by painted motifs (figures 49 and 57). Yet more elaborate decoration can be seen on vessels decorated to represent the god Bes during that period. Either depicting only his head, with leonine features and mane, or his head and

**14.** (Left) Fine Nile-silt, blue-painted vessel; Valley of the Kings, late Eighteenth Dynasty. (Courtesy of Metropolitan Museum of Art, Gift of Theodore M. Davis, 1909; 09.184.83.)
**15.** (Right) Blue-painted Nile-silt Bes vase; late Eighteenth to early Nineteenth Dynasties. (Courtesy of Ägyptisches Museum, Berlin; 22620.)

dwarf-like body, a combination of applied, painted and modelled techniques was used. Bes vases executed in these techniques were manufactured throughout the Third Intermediate and Late Periods (figure 61). Mould-made heads, probably representing the goddess Hathor, were added to the sides of bowls during the New Kingdom and some animals were also depicted using modelling techniques. Most common were the gazelle or ibex, the heads and necks of which were hand-modelled and added to the necks of some vessels, mainly two-handled amphorae. On occasion the body of the animal might be painted on the upper part of the vessel; there are rare examples of the entire body of an animal, either an ibex or a calf, hand-modelled and applied to a vessel (figure 63). These representations usually occur on vessels with blue-painted decoration; others with this same colour scheme were ornamented with applied decoration in the form of floral motifs or hieroglyphs. Some shallow bowls were decorated to resemble ducks, having a hand-modelled representation of the bird's head on one side and the tail at the other. Exceptional for their early date and extreme rarity are fragments, possibly from a large stand, now reconstructed, decorated with applied representations of dogs, a tied lotus and part of the back of a lion. These seem to date to the Old Kingdom and were discovered by Petrie at Koptos; they are now in the Petrie Museum, University College London (UC 34867).

**Burnishing**
While the techniques of both polishing and burnishing improved the appearance of the surface, actual designs seem to have

**16.** Blue-painted Nile-silt amphora with applied ibex head and body painted on shoulder; Malkata, late Eighteenth Dynasty. (Courtesy of Metropolitan Museum of Art, Rogers Fund, 1911; 11.215.460.)

been effected only by burnishing. This is encountered in the form of lines of burnish radiating from the centre of bowls in the Archaic Period (figure 25), or bands of burnish on the rims of bowls during the New Kingdom.

## Fenestration

Fenestration was not a common decorative technique. It occurs periodically in the sides of some tall stands or pot supports from the Old Kingdom onwards, while there are a few examples of deep, ornamental bowls from the New Kingdom with sections of the wall cut away. This technique was executed when the vessel was in a leather-hard state before firing.

## Incision

Incised decoration is encountered mainly from the Middle Kingdom and Second Intermediate Period and then more frequently on vessels made in marl-clay fabrics. Designs were executed with the aid of sharp tools such as metal knives, split reeds and combs to produce straight or undulating lines, dots (often called punctates) and V shapes (figures 34, 35, 45). Occasionally these designs were filled in with white pigment after the vessel was fired, while the designs themselves were executed before it was fired (figure 4).

## Modelling of the vessel wall

Modelling of the vessel wall most frequently took the form of manipulating it to produce designs, or parts of designs, with the fingers and was done before firing, when the clay was still moist. This technique was used mainly from the New Kingdom onwards. The motifs consist primarily of faces of the goddess Hathor (figure 54) and the god Bes, which were modelled out from the interior of the vessel, either in its neck or upper body. Representations of Bes frequently have some details of the face and the arms applied to the vessel wall. Such vessels often have painted designs. Modelling of the vessel wall was also used to emphasise painted motifs as in the case of an impressive goblet now in the British Museum (figure 17). The lower part is decorated in imitation of a white lotus, the petals of which are also modelled out from the wall, as are the figures of the kneeling god, Heh, the falcons and the hieroglyphs on the upper part. It is painted in blue, red and black. During the New Kingdom the walls of some bowls were modelled with indentations while others had sections of the wall folded inwards. Finally, the occurrence of

*Egyptian Pottery*

**17.** Large lotus-shaped chalice decorated with falcons flanking the god Heh (Eternity) and hieroglyphs; Eighteenth to Nineteenth Dynasties. (British Museum, 47380/1.)

ribbing in the exterior surface, perhaps best included as an aspect of modelled decoration, may be mentioned. It is known from the Late Period onwards and was produced either as part of the throwing process or before the vessel was fired.

## Painting

The technique of painting on pottery was mastered by the Egyptians during the Predynastic Period but during the Dynastic Period it is encountered with any frequency only from the late Second Intermediate Period to the New Kingdom. Two basic techniques were used: decoration applied before firing and decoration applied after firing. In both cases designs were applied with a brush, while some designs executed after firing were applied using fingers. Brushes were made from reeds of different thickness, the ends of which were pounded to provide bristles.

Pre-firing decoration employed pigments which could withstand exposure to the heat of the kiln. These consisted of the colours red and black, which were derived from oxides of iron (ochres) and manganese, and blue, derived from cobalt. Not all of these were used together in each period. Simple linear designs or spots of colour in monochrome red or brown occur intermittently from the Archaic Period to the Late Period. From the Archaic Period are some examples of horned animals and birds

**18.** (Above left) Blue-painted Nile-silt jar with horse motif; mid Eighteenth Dynasty. (Courtesy of Ägyptisches Museum, Berlin; 14412.)
**19.** (Above right) Blue-painted Nile-silt jar with floral collar; Amarna, late Eighteenth Dynasty. (Courtesy of Ägyptisches Museum, Berlin; 15352.)
**20.** (Right) Blue-painted Nile-silt bowl with lotus and papyrus motifs; Luxor, late Eighteenth Dynasty. (Courtesy of Metropolitan Museum of Art, gift of the Earl of Carnarvon, 1923; 23.7.3.)

while in the Second Intermediate Period bird and plant motifs
were reintroduced. During the first half of the Eighteenth
Dynasty linear and floral designs were executed in red and black,
and during the middle of the Eighteenth Dynasty faunal motifs
were incorporated. Linear decoration in black continued.

Painted decoration employing blue, red and black is encountered only from the middle of the Eighteenth Dynasty onwards;
the blue pigment predominates. This pigment was made by the
Egyptians using only a very small amount of cobalt, less than 0.5
per cent, and may have been derived from deposits of alum which
occur in the oases of Kharga and Dakhleh. Mainly floral motifs
were used, though a wide range of other motifs was incorporated.
This form of decoration was inspired by the practice of festooning
actual floral garlands around pottery vessels on festive occasions.
It occurs in combination with all the other decorative techniques
and is the most complex decorated pottery to have been produced
by the dynastic Egyptians. It may be termed *blue-painted pottery.*

Post-firing decoration was much rarer than that painted before
firing. A wider colour palette was employed: blue, black, red,
green and yellow, normally applied over a white coating. The
blue and green paints derive their colour from a synthetic
pigment coloured by copper, called frit, which produces a more
intense colour when applied in thick layers. During the Middle
Kingdom azurite was used as a blue pigment. The red and black
are ochres of iron, black also being made from soot; the yellow is
derived from ochre or orpiment and the white from gypsum or
chalk. This type of painted decoration, which may be termed
*polychrome decoration,* is known mainly from the Middle and
New Kingdoms; during the former it is encountered primarily on
the interior of bowls while in the latter on jars and handled
vessels. Polychrome painted decoration does not have the
tenacity of that fired on to the pot and occurs primarily on vessels
intended for the tomb. The large new Kingdom amphorae with
this type of decoration known from domestic contexts may have
been used on festive occasions only. Designs of spots and crosses,
executed with the fingers, and bands, all in white, were painted
on to bowls or jars after firing during the Middle Kingdom and
Second Intermediate Period. There are a few post-firing decorated bowls known from the late Old Kingdom with monochrome
designs. Painted decoration occurs more frequently than that
executed in other techniques but even so it was not common by
comparison with the quantity of undecorated pottery which was
manufactured.

**21.** Blue-painted Nile silt jar with faunal motifs; late Eighteenth Dynasty. (Courtesy of Brooklyn Museum, Wilbour Fund; 59.2.)

**22.** Polychrome decorated, handled vessels, fine marl clay, tomb of Kha; Deir el-Medina, late Eighteenth Dynasty. (Courtesy of Il Museo delle Antichita Egilze, Turin.)

# 4
# Historical development

The development of both the shape and the decoration of Egyptian pottery throughout the period under review and the materials used are now much better understood as a result of intense research since the mid 1960s. The methods used in ascertaining this development have been quite varied. Principally they depend upon the isolation of deposits of pottery from tombs or settlements which can be securely dated to particular periods by means of their association with inscribed material giving the names of individual rulers, groups of rulers, or persons whose historical placing is known. In some cases such information is written on or incised into the pots themselves (figures 26, 52). Once these deposits have been isolated their characteristics can be studied and vessels from contexts which lack inscribed material can be dated by comparison with them. Much pioneering work in this field was carried out by archaeologists at the end of the nineteeth century and the beginning of the twentieth. Foremost amongst them was Sir W. M. F. Petrie, who has been called 'Father of Egyptian Archaeology' and the 'Father of Pots'. Changes in ancient Egyptian ceramics occurred gradually and rarely do they coincide neatly with the main periods of Egyptian history. A great similarity between the shapes of vessels made from clay and those made from stone and metal occurs during all periods and foreign imports also influenced the potter.

## The Archaic Period (Dynasties I to II)

The pottery of this first phase of Egyptian history is best known from the royal cemeteries at Abydos and Saqqara. It is a direct development of that known from the late Predynastic Period in terms of shape, materials and surface finish, although painted decoration was less common. The latter is encountered on cylindrical jars which bear a lattice design, imitating rope slings in which pottery was carried, and on squat jars in the form of groups of straight or wavy lines, commas and spots. A few vessels have more elaborate painted designs which include birds and horned animals. Applied decoration was inspired by bands of string which were used to support the pots when they were drying, the impressions of which can be seen on some vessels. Decorative burnishing occurs on the interior of some bowls. Undulating lines modelled into the upper part of cylindrical jars are the last echo

**23.** (Above) Nile-silt *(centre and centre right)* and fine marl-clay vessels; Archaic Period. (Courtesy of Macquarie University; MU 979, 1508, 1537, 1698, 2219.)

**24.** (Below left) Squat fine marl-clay jar with maroon decoration; Hu (?), First Dynasty. (Courtesy of National Gallery of Victoria; NGV D115/1982.)

**25.** (Below right) Bowl in fine marl clay with decorative burnish; Hu, First Dynasty. (Courtesy of National Gallery of Victoria; NGV D112/1982.)

of the influence on Egyptian potters of the wavy-ledge handles on vessels imported from Palestine during the Predynastic Period.

Large storage jars with an elongated profile typify the ceramics of the period, as do the cylindrical and squat jars. Large jars from the tombs of the royal family and their retainers often have royal names incised into them. Vessels made from marl clays became more common, with polished surfaces imitating alabaster (figure 23, left).

## The Old Kingdom (Dynasties III to VI) and First Intermediate Period (Dynasties VII to early XI)

The ceramics of the Old Kingdom, also called the Pyramid Age, fall into two broad groups: fine wares with coated and/or burnished or polished surfaces, and coarser wares with uncoated surfaces. The latter consist of common household shapes such as

**26.** Large Nile-silt jar with incised name of King Narmer; Tarkhan, First Dynasty. (Courtesy of Petrie Museum; UC 16083.)
**27.** (Below) Old Kingdom bread mould, straw-tempered Nile-silt clay; Akhmim. (Courtesy of Dr N. Kanawati; Macquarie University 2271.)

**28.** Nile-silt Meydum bowl and jar, red-coated and polished; Matmar, Fifth Dynasty. (Courtesy of National Gallery of Victoria; NGV 3358A.3, 3358B.3.)

**29.** Deep spouted bowl, fine marl clay; El-Kab, Fourth Dynasty. (Courtesy of Petrie Museum; UC 17844.)

**30.** Squat, spouted jar, black fired and polished Nile silt; Deshasheh, Fifth Dynasty. (Courtesy of Petrie Museum; UC 17750.)

**31.** (Above left) Necked jar, black fired and polished Nile silt; Fourth to Fifth Dynasties. (Courtesy of Petrie Museum; UC 15738.)
**32.** (Above right) Squat, necked jar, fine marl clay; Dendera, First Intermediate Period. (Courtesy of National Gallery of Victoria; NGV 729.2.)
**33.** (Below) Nile-silt jars, First Intermediate Period; *left to right,* provenance unknown (MU 958), Sedment (MU 1672), Gurob (MU 946), Abydos (MU 1520). (Courtesy of Macquarie University.)

bread moulds, dishes and jars, the former of table wares and some storage vessels. The commonest surface coating was a red slip, often polished or burnished, which was applied to vessels made from both Nile silt and marl clays, though black polished surfaces also occur. Painted decoration almost completely disappeared, though a few very interesting bowls decorated after firing are known from the late Old Kingdom. They depict motifs seen in wall paintings, including the hunt, and have been found mainly at Aswan. Typical forms in fine wares include deep basins and necked jars (ewers), sharply carinated bowls (often called Meydum bowls after a site where they were found in abundance; figure 28), bowls with applied spouts and squat jars often with a spout and carination (nicknamed teapots). Spouts were also produced by modelling the rim. One of the best dated groups of Old Kingdom pottery comes from the tomb of Queen Hetepheres, the mother of Khufu, builder of the Great Pyramid at Giza. The period is marked by a uniformity of ceramic products throughout the country.

The ensuing First Intermediate Period was a period of disunity following the collapse of the central administration and its ceramic products display regional variations. The sharply carinated bowl disappeared, to be replaced by others with rounded or straight sides, while small jars with bag-shaped bodies and others with tapering or sharply pointed lower bodies and bases developed.

## The Middle Kingdom (Dynasties late XI to XII) and Second Intermediate Period (Dynasties XIII to XVII)

Egypt was reunited under one rule in the middle of the Eleventh Dynasty and by the early Twelfth Dynasty had entered another period of prosperity and stable government. This is reflected in the ceramic repertoire, which may be divided into three phases. During the first of these, from the late Eleventh to the early Twelfth Dynasty, regional variations continued, while in the second, covering the mid Twelfth Dynasty, and the third, from the late Twelfth to the Thirteenth Dynasty, uniformity throughout most of the country re-emerged. This three-phase division of the pottery is a result of the work by Dr Dorothea Arnold.

Some of the characteristics of the period as a whole may be summarised as follows. Common amongst the marls used was a dense-bodied, fine clay; vessels made from it frequently have incised and applied decoration. The incised designs comprise

**34.** (Above) Marl-clay footed bowl, incised and applied decoration; El-Kab, early Twelfth Dynasty. (Courtesy of Petrie Museum; UC 18422.)

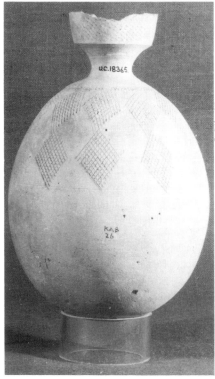

**35.** (Left) Fine marl-clay water jar, incised decoration; El-Kab, early Twelfth Dynasty. (Courtesy of Petrie Museum; UC 18365.)

**36.** (Below) Small Nile-silt jar with quatre-foil mouth; El-Kab, Twelfth Dynasty. (Courtesy of Petrie Museum; UC 18327.)

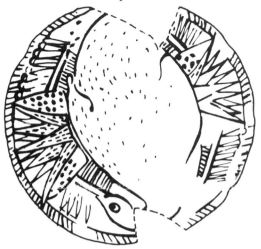

37. Polychrome decorated bowl with trussed goose on flowers; Beni Hasan, Middle Kingdom. (After Garstang, J., *The Burial Customs of Ancient Egypt*, figure 143.)

straight or wavy lines, commas and lozenges filled with cross-hatching. Femino-form vases with applied faces, arms and breasts occur first during the Middle Kingdom. The late Twelfth Dynasty saw the beginning of a tradition, which was to last until the New Kingdom, of painting bands of colour (red, black or white) on the body or rim of a wide range of shapes. Jars with undulating necks began to be manufactured while others with four spouts modelled into the rim (quatrefoil mouths) appeared. Some open bowls,

38. Nile-silt vessels; Dendera, Middle Kingdom. (Courtesy of National Gallery of Victoria, NGV D123/1982, D116/1982, D122/1982.)

**39.** Nile-silt footed cup; Sedment, early Twelfth Dynasty. (Courtesy of Petrie Museum; UC 18182.)

mostly found in graves, received elaborate polychrome decoration, with motifs of birds (figure 37), plants, humans, stars and geometric designs, which are similar to those found in tomb reliefs. Characteristic shapes include hemispherical bowls, stemmed cups, medium-sized jars with pronounced flaring necks and large necked jars with thickened rims. Distinctions between fine table wares and coarse domestic wares continued. Shallow open bread dishes dating from the late Middle Kingdom or Thirteenth Dynasty often have incised designs on their interiors.

With the collapse of the Middle Kingdom, regional variations again emerged and the ceramics of the Second Intermediate

**40.** Burnished marl-clay jar imitating alabaster; El-Kab, early Twelfth Dynasty. (Courtesy of Petrie Museum; UC 18371.)

Period appear to be divisible into early and late phases. Major studies on the pottery from Upper and Middle Egypt have been carried out by Janine Bourriau and on that from the Delta by Dr Manfred Bietak. However, despite internal rival factions, trade within the country flourished, as did that with Cyprus and the Levant, attested by the occurrence of pottery from these regions in Egypt. Marl clays, coarser than those of the Middle Kingdom, were used more frequently and incised and applied decoration became commoner. As the period progressed painted decoration, either in reddish brown or black, became more elaborate, with groups of straight or diagonal lines, often intersecting, occurring on squat, carinated jars, though simple painted rim bands were still in fashion. Occasionally depictions of birds or plants are found. This decoration was possibly influenced by Palestinian and Cypriot wares. While hemispherical bowls became deeper and the quatrefoil mouth disappeared, femino-form vases continued to be made. Drop-shaped vases and bottles with slender, flaring necks appeared.

During the Second Intermediate Period small juglets were manufactured in black-fired wares, often with lustrous surfaces

**41.** Early Eleventh Dynasty Nile-silt bowl, Hu (E.217.1899); Twelfth Dynasty Nile-silt and marl-clay jars and stands, Hu (E.94. 1902, E.105. 1902, E.250.1899, E.111-112.1902), and tall stand, Beni Hasan (E.176.1902). (Courtesy of Fitzwilliam Museum, Cambridge.)

**42.** (Left) Elaborate necked marl-clay jar, incised designs; Qurna, late Second Intermediate Period. (Courtesy of Petrie Museum; UC 18252.)
**43.** (Right) Nile-silt necked jar, red-coated and burnished; late Second Intermediate Period. (Courtesy of Macquarie University; MU 863.)

and incised punctate designs in zigzag lines which were commonly filled in with white. These have been termed Tell el-Yahudiyeh wares, after a site where a large quantity was found. Juglets in these wares, although known from Egypt, the Levant and Cyprus, were made only in Egypt and the Levant. During the Thirteenth Dynasty other shapes were also made, namely vases in the form of fish and birds (figure 4). The latter seem to have been hand-modelled and not wheel-made.

## The New Kingdom (Dynasties XVIII to XX)

Campaigning on the part of the rulers of the late Seventeenth and early Eighteenth Dynasties, who belonged to a family which originated in Luxor, again brought Egypt under the rule of one king. Foreigners who had ruled in the Delta, the so-called Hyksos, were expelled and Egyptian influence was exerted over

**44.** Grey-fired Nile-silt juglet with punctate designs; Second Intermediate Period. (Courtesy of Petrie Museum; UC 13468.)

the Levant and the Sudan. Throughout the Eighteenth Dynasty a lively trade network with these two regions flourished, also embracing Cyprus, Crete and Greece, and a period of great prosperity followed. Large quantities of pottery, used as containers for such trade items as wine, oil and opium, were brought into Egypt, influencing the development of the local ceramics and resulting in the manufacture of direct imitations. The period is characterised by the manufacture of many fancy forms and an increase in the use of decoration.

While the ceramic traditions of the late Second Intermediate Period continued into the early Eighteenth Dynasty, during the first part of that dynasty new ones emerged. Broad, round-bodied, two-handled jars (amphorae) were manufactured in

**45.** Black-fired Nile-silt fish vase with punctate designs; Tell el-Yahudiyeh, Thirteenth Dynasty. (Courtesy of Petrie Museum; UC 13477.)

**46.** Nile-silt vessels; first half of the Eighteenth Dynasty. (Courtesy of Macquarie University; MU 988, 1466, 1468, 1504, 1528, 1605.)

imitation of those imported from the Levant, while handles were added to squat carinated jars, which increased in size. Jars with biconical and pear-shaped bodies, red-coated and polished surfaces, with painted decoration of bands of colour, continued to be in vogue. This simple monochrome painting gradually gave way to designs in red and black in which stylised floral motifs were incorporated and eventually also representations of birds, gazelles and cattle. This type of decoration is encountered mostly on jars similar in shape to those of the preceding period but with taller necks and on a pale background colour. Femino-form vases lost their applied arms and were generally painted; incised decoration and painted rim bands became less common. Fine-quality marl clays were used once again for table wares and cosmetic jars. Figure vases in the form of nurses, female musicians and animals are amongst the finest products of the period.

**47.** Red polished figure vases; mid Eighteenth Dynasty. (Courtesy of Ägyptisches Museum, Berlin; left to right, 14476, 14152, 13155, 13156.)

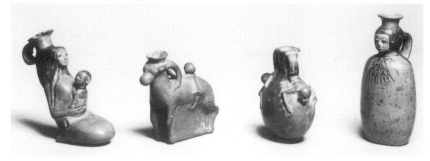

**48.** (Right) Fine marl-clay jug, decorated in red and black; mid Eighteenth Dynasty. (Courtesy of Petrie Museum; UC 8918.)
**49.** (Below left) Blue-painted femino-form Nile-silt vase with bovine motifs; applied face at rim and breasts visible on right profile. Saqqara (?), Eighteenth to Nineteenth Dynasties. (Courtesy of Art Museum, Princeton University; 52.87.)
**50.** (Below right) Red and black painted Nile-silt jar with gazelle motif; mid Eighteenth Dynasty. (Courtesy of Petrie Museum; UC 8703.)

**51.** (Above) Small Nile-silt polychrome decorated jar depicting a duck; Abydos, mid to late Eighteenth Dynasty. (Courtesy of Ashmolean Museum; E 2434.)

**52.** (Above right) Inscribed marl-clay wine jars (amphorae), tomb of Tutankhamun; Valley of the Kings, late Eighteenth Dynasty. (Courtesy of Griffith Institute, Ashmolean Museum.)

**53.** (Below) Typical late Eighteenth Dynasty Nile-silt vessels; Malkata.

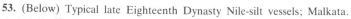

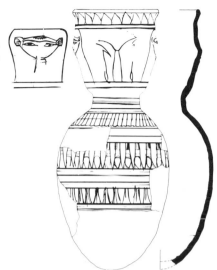

**54.** Blue-painted jar with floral motifs and face of Hathor; Malkata, late Eighteenth Dynasty.

Gradually this repertoire was superseded by yet another during the second half of the Eighteenth Dynasty and this lasted with few changes for the rest of the New Kingdom. It is typified by finds from the sites of Malkata and Amarna. Amphorae either became slenderer or received angular shoulders. Very large jars with flaring necks were manufactured as were others of smaller size with globular bodies. Tall, slender, one-handled bottles became more common (figure 22). A marl clay with a cream polished or burnished surface was frequently used for amphorae, handled bottles and small, two-handled lentoid flasks (pilgrim flasks). The manufacture of figure vases ceased and painted decoration in red and black was generally replaced by blue-painted pottery. While some motifs occur in both styles of

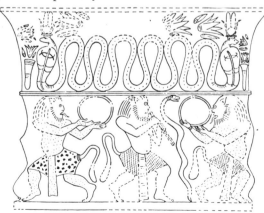

**55.** Blue-painted stand (?) with Bes the Musician and cobra goddess; Deir el-Medina, Nineteenth Dynasty. (After Bruyère, B., *Fouilles de Deir el Médineh [1933-4]*, figure 49.)

**56.** (Above) Polychrome decorated jar and amphorae; Deir el-Medina, Nineteenth Dynasty. (Courtesy of Ägyptisches Museum, Berlin; 21326, 21325, 21327.)
**57.** (Below left) Large Nile-silt femino-form vase with floral and human motifs in brown; Nineteenth Dynasty. (Courtesy of Petrie Museum; UC 8696.)
**58.** (Below centre) Nile-silt jar with modelled Bes image; Nineteenth Dynasty. (Courtesy of Petrie Museum; UC 19228.)
**59.** (Below right) Red coated and polished Nile-silt jar; Twenty-Sixth Dynasty. (Courtesy of Trustees of the British Museum; 58283.)

**60.** Nile-silt jug; Late Period. (Courtesy of Macquarie University; MU 1773.)

painted pottery, that with blue is far more elaborate and less stylised. A wide range of techniques was used and though floral motifs dominated (figures 15, 19, 20) others incorporating fauna (birds, cattle, fish, gazelles, ibexes, horses, cats [figures 16, 18, 21]), humans and hieroglyphs occur (figure 17). The goddess Hathor is depicted, as is Bes (figure 15) and rarely a cobra goddess. Polychrome decoration, encountered rarely from the mid Eighteenth Dynasty, became more common, mainly on amphorae and some jars. Small amphorae with elaborate polychrome decoration are known during the Nineteenth to Twentieth Dynasties. Material of this latter period has been found in abundance at Deir el-Medina.

### The Third Intermediate Period (Dynasties XXI to XXIV) and the Late Period (Dynasties XXV to XXXI)

The pottery of the last seven hundred years before the conquest of Egypt by Alexander the Great is among the least defined of all, though studies of material from several Delta sites, such as Mendes and Tell el-Maskhuta, from Saqqara and from Karnak are beginning to clarify the picture. Dr Jacquet-Gordon has identified two ceramic phases amongst the material from Karnak. one extending from the Twenty-First Dynasty to the Twent:

**61.** Jars with Bes image; *centre and left,* marl clay, Late Period (UC 2888, 2877); *right,* Nile silt, Third Intermediate Period (UC 36313). (Courtesy of Petrie Museum.)

Fifth and another from the Twenty-Sixth to the Thirty-First, which extends into the following Ptolemaic Period. Some overlapping of the two occurs.

During the first of these phases the pottery resembles that of the late New Kingdom, though painted decoration disappeared almost completely and marl clays were less commonly used. Vases decorated with the image of Bes continued to be made, but much reduced in size and schematically treated. Tall slender jars with undulating bodies tended to replace the amphorae. During the second phase vessels made from marl clays were manufactured in greater abundance and new shapes developed, some of which were inspired by vessels imported from other Mediterranean countries, particularly Greece. Greek trading colonies were now located in the Egyptian Delta and Greek mercenaries were employed in the Egyptian army. Decoration on small Bes jars became more elaborate and painted designs in monochrome, black or reddish brown, with linear and floral motifs, appeared. These occur most often on very deep bowls with pronounced ledge rims. Large jars with long, undulating bodies appeared, as did handled jars with bulbous bodies and complex rim formations.

# 5
# The functions of pottery

Many methods are available to us when attempting to define the functions served by pottery vessels in ancient Egyptian society. We have the vessels themselves, features of which can give some indication of the functions for which they were used, for example general size, width of mouth and neck, the existence of spouts or handles and the quality of manufacture, material used and type of surface finish. In some cases the contents held by vessels can be determined not only from any remains found within them but also from inscriptions on them (figure 52). In addition, vessels made from pottery, frequently coloured red, are depicted in scenes which decorate tombs and temples, with captions giving us the names which were used for specific shapes. Some other texts refer in passing to the use of pottery vessels. The find contexts can also provide indications of their function. The functions of pottery can be grouped into three main categories: daily life, religious activities and funerary practices. The potter was conscious of the function his products were to serve and this determined his selection of raw materials, his treatment of them, the surface finish applied and the details of the shapes made.

**Daily life**

Clay was the principal material of vessels which were used in a wide range of domestic activities by all strata of society, which accounts for the vast output of the ancient potters. Foremost amongst these were the preparation of food and drink, their serving and storage. In general, common Nile silt clay was used for domestic vessels such as cups, bowls, dishes and jars. Coloured surface coatings were often applied to those used in the consumption of food, and surface compaction and coatings on those used for storing beverages and valued commodities such as oils and perfumes. An exception to this was the exploitation of the porous nature of Nile silt clay in the manufacture of water jars, the evaporation of some of the contents through the wall of the vessel serving to cool the remainder. Marl clays were often used for jars used in the storage and transport of fluids, frequently with coated or compacted surfaces. The diversity of shapes produced for domestic use is indicated by the illustrations in this book. As well as their use in individual households, storage jars were necessary in abundance for use in the storerooms

**62.** (Above) Spouted femino-form Nile-silt milk vase; early Eighteenth Dynasty. (Courtesy of Petrie Museum; UC 8459.)

**63.** (Right) Large ornamental blue-painted Nile-silt amphora with lid; late Eighteenth Dynasty. (Courtesy of Museum of Fine Arts, Boston; 64.9.)

connected with the large estates. A striking feature of much Egyptian pottery is the occurrence of round and pointed bases rather than flat ones. Ancient floors were frequently rough, sand-covered or made from earth and round or pointed bases could be nestled into these uneven surfaces. Pottery was often simply supported against walls or placed in wooden or pottery supports. To enable vessels with round or pointed bases to stand safely on solid surfaces, such as tables, pottery stands were used. Domestic pottery does not seem to have had much value, being easily obtainable, and its cost would have been very low. Decorated vessels, those with more elaborate shapes or imported ones may have had a greater value because of their comparative scarcity and been more available to the wealthier members of society. Elaborately decorated vessels, such as those of the New Kingdom, may have been reserved for use on festive occasions

**64.** Satirical sketch of mouse, attended by cats; Nineteenth Dynasty. (After Brunner-Traut, E., *Die Alten Ägypter*, figure 43.)

and some examples from that period undoubtedly had an ornamental use, as is indicated by more complex decoration on one side than the other.

Pottery vessels were also used in connection with various other crafts and trades and the transport of farm produce and, particularly, wine throughout the country. The latter was greatly facilitated by the addition of handles to vessels. Large jars used for carrying wine had their mouths sealed by mud caps to prevent loss of their contents; those placed in tombs or used for long-term storage were also sealed in this way (figure 52). Pottery lids were used for others when there was less likelihood of their being dislodged.

The surfaces of some vessels and fragments of broken vessels (sherds) were used by artists as a medium for sketches and a whole genre of informal art. Scribes also used sherds as a cheap writing material, as did students in schools.

**65.** Artist's sketches, horse's head and crowned falcon in ink on a jar; Amarna, late Eighteenth Dynasty.

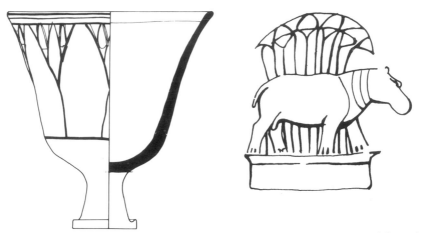

**66.** (Left) Blue-painted chalice in the form of a blue lotus flower; Amarna, late Eighteenth Dynasty. (British Museum 58461.)
**67.** (Right) Drawing of a sacred hippopotamus on a jar; Amarna, late Eighteenth Dynasty.

## Religious activities

An important component of the ceremonies performed in temples and shrines throughout Egypt was the ritual pouring of water libations to the gods, symbolising the offering to them of water and other beverages which they required for their well-being. This act was also a token of man's thanks for supplying him with the necessities of his existence. Whilst this was commonly done from specific shapes made from metal, examples in pottery are known from all periods. Scenes in tombs and on stelae show that libations could be poured into chalices in the shape of the blue lotus flower made from pottery, metal and faience. Such chalices also held offerings of flowers. Special loaves of bread were included amongst the offerings to the gods and the dead, the thin cylindrical shape of which was derived from the pottery moulds in which they were baked. Moulds of this shape are found associated only with the remains of temples. The burning of incense represented the offering of food to the gods and was done in bowls, made from pottery as well as metal, often on stands to which they might be attached. Such acts were performed normally by the king and priesthood. There are rare examples of jars decorated with sketches of a particular god or sacred animal, which, like some of the elaborate vases with representations of Hathor and Bes, may have been used in their worship. They may also have had a votive function as is the case with a small number of bowls found at Abydos, the cult centre of Osiris, god of resurrection, which bear drawings of Osiris and other gods.

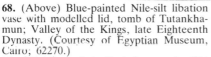

**68.** (Above) Blue-painted Nile-silt libation vase with modelled lid, tomb of Tutankhamun; Valley of the Kings, late Eighteenth Dynasty. (Courtesy of Egyptian Museum, Cairo; 62270.)
**69.** (Right) Archaic Period or early Old Kingdom pot burial. (Courtesy of Petrie Museum; UC 14856-7.)

## Funerary practices

As a result of their belief in a life after death which was essentially the same as that on earth, the Egyptians furnished the burials of their dead with the objects of daily life. Amongst these were various quantities of pottery vessels, the majority of which were drawn from that made for the use of the living. Most of the vessels illustrated in this book were found in tombs, where they have been much better preserved than those from settlements. In addition to those of a domestic nature other vessels, which were used in religious ceremonies such as pouring libations, were included. These enabled the deceased to make offerings to the gods in the afterlife. Such vessels were also used by priests during the rites which accompanied the interment of the deceased person. On this occasion pottery jars which contained milk or water were ritually broken at the entrance of the tomb. Pottery vessels were used to contain offerings to the dead made by priests

**70.** Inscribed Nile-silt canopic jars with modelled human-headed lids; *right,* Abydos (?), (E.17.1950), and *left,* Sedment, (E.40.1921), mid Eighteenth Dynasty. (Courtesy of Fitzwilliam Museum, Cambridge.)

or members of the dead person's family at the tomb. At various times throughout Egyptian history burials themselves were made in large pottery jars or basins.

Some forms were made specifically for burial with the dead. Foremost amongst these were examples in pottery of the jars used to hold certain internal organs of a person whose body had been mummified; these organs were removed during the process of mummification and had to be buried along with the body. These vessels are called canopic jars and their lids took the form either of human heads or of representations of those of the guardian genii who protected these organs.

Jars of pottery were also used to hold small figures (*shabtis*) which would perform manual labour in place of the deceased if he or she was called upon to do so. Other vessels of pottery found in tombs were decorated in imitation of those made from stone. A class of crudely made miniature vessels is known from tombs as are others called dummy vases, which are solid. These categories of vessel would, through magic, have functioned as full-size actual vessels in the afterlife. Magical practices also account for the occurrence of letters addressed to the dead written in ink on pottery bowls, and the so-called Execration Texts, also written upon bowls. In these the enemy was vilified and the bowl was broken to symbolise his defeat or destruction. It is possible that the jars and handled vessels of the New Kingdom with polychrome decoration were intended primarily for inclusion in the tomb. Some vessels which were blue-painted before firing, and probably intended for domestic use, received polychrome decoration and inscriptions signifying their conversion to a funerary use (figure 56).

# 6
# The role of pottery
# in the study of ancient Egypt

Given the vast quantity of pottery which survives, with collections
in many major museums throughout the world, and the ever
increasing volume being unearthed by carefully controlled
excavations, pottery has a significant role to play in the study of
ancient Egypt. Archaeologists now work with specialists in other
fields in bringing new scientific techniques and differing skills to
bear on the problems they are investigating. A few examples will
serve to illustrate the uses to which pottery is put in Egyptology
and the techniques which are adopted.

**Technology**

The study of the raw materials which were used in the
manufacture of pottery and the techniques of its formation,
decoration and firing contributes to the understanding of ancient
technology. The potters of ancient Egypt appreciated fully the
characteristics and limitations of their raw materials and had
mastered their exploitation from a very early date. As has been
mentioned previously, they understood the suitability of certain
types of clay for the manufacture of particular shapes of vessels
which were to serve different functions. In addition to the
application of surface treatments to make their fired clay bodies
more efficient, the potters altered their raw materials in various
ways to this end also. By the process of levigation they improved
the homogeneity and workability of the clay and removed
extraneous inclusions which might have a detrimental effect on
the strength of the vessel during firing. On the other hand, by
adding additional tempering material they could provide a more
open texture, lower the firing temperature and alter the firing
characteristics of the clays. Different types of clay could be mixed
to produce material with new characteristics, thus extending the
potter's range of clay types.

The exact composition of the various clays and the identification of inclusions can be determined in a variety of ways. Tests
have been carried out on clays available today in Egypt and their
properties identified; the fired fabrics of vessels made from these
clays have been compared with those produced in antiquity.
Neutron activation analyses, X-ray techniques, chemical tests and

the use of high-powered microscopes to identify crystalline structure and the exact nature of the components have enabled a detailed characterisation of the ancient materials. The sorting of examples of pottery analysed in this way into groups which represent those made from similar clay types has in some cases been done with the aid of computers. Tests carried out on the pigments which were used in the decoration of pottery have shown a high level of sophistication in their use and manufacture, particularly in the synthesis of various pigments to supplement those available in nature. The use of natural and synthetic pigments required a complete understanding not only of their nature and their reactions to heat, but also of how they would react when applied to clay bodies and fired on to them.

The understanding of both the chemical and the physical reactions to heat was essential when the most sensitive and crucial stage of pottery manufacture was reached — the firing. If too little heat is applied the clay body will be fragile and susceptible to the effects of water: if too much, the surface will bloat, vitrify and slump as the fabric gradually changes to a molten state. Efficient pyrotechnology necessitated the design of suitable kilns which enable the heat and air to circulate, separation of the pots from the fire itself, control of the air intake and fuel to produce the correct atmosphere (an oxidising atmosphere) to enable all carbon to be burnt out and an optimum firing obtained. All of these were mastered by the Egyptian potters, who were highly competent craftsmen, completely in control of all these variables. This can also be seen from their deft manipulation of the simple potters' wheels they used for the majority of their manufactures and their control of the centrifugal forces produced during the rotation of these wheels.

## Dating and trade

'Once settle the pottery of a country, and the key is in our hands for all future explorations. A simple glance at a mound of ruins, even without dismounting, will show as much to anyone who knows the styles of the pottery, as weeks of work may reveal to a beginner.'

This observation made in 1891 by Petrie in the report on his excavation at Tell el-Hesy in Palestine indicates the importance the study of pottery played in his assessment of the dating of ancient sites. In this he was a pioneer not only in Palestine but also Egypt, where he spent most of his working life.

The study of pottery as a tool in the dating of sites, individual

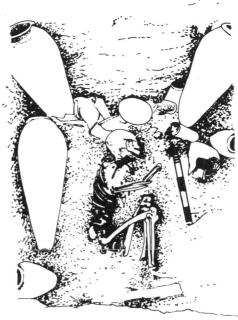

**71.** Early First Dynasty burial with pottery vessels which enable its dating; Saqqara. (After Emery, W. B., *Archaic Egypt,* plate 22.)

strata on a site and burials is perhaps its most common use by archaeologists. This use is not surprising as there are very few sites of any kind which do not provide large quantities of pottery. The principal characteristics of the pottery of the main periods of Egyptian history have now been determined. With this information it is possible to analyse the pottery from most contexts and suggest a reasonably secure dating, or range of dates, for the material. This method of dating is used in conjunction with information derived from any inscriptions and other objects found in the deposit. As well as providing dating evidence for a site, pottery can indicate the activities carried out on some sites or parts of them. This can be done by determining the frequency of certain types in relation to others, especially when the predominant type served a specific function. Examples of this might be the identification of large numbers of bread moulds in an area, indicating the existence of a bakery, or of large storage or water jars, indicating storerooms or areas used for the communal water supply.

Pottery can also be used to identify an Egyptian presence or contact with Egypt in regions outside that country. At various times throughout history the Egyptians expanded their sphere of influence into such regions as Nubia, the Sudan, Palestine and the Sahara. Whether creating settlements of their own or living in those of the locals, the Egyptians often left evidence of their presence in the form of Egyptian-made objects, including pottery. As pottery containers for various commodities were used in trade with neighbouring countries, their occurrence on sites outside Egypt can also be used to document ancient trading networks.

In the study of the varying strength of the earth's magnetic field in history, Egyptian ceramics from well dated contexts have been used to provide data. Clay becomes magnetised during its formation into vessels and firing and the intensity of the magnetic field at the time of those processes can be determined. Results obtained from pottery and mud bricks have shown the magnetic field in Egypt to have fluctuated considerably during the first three millenia BC, the period studied.


**Decorative arts**

In the study of ancient Egyptian decorative arts pottery also has a role to play. Changes in fashion and taste affected the potters as much as other craftsmen, all of whom worked within the general framework of Egyptian artistic conventions. While the vast quantity of Egyptian pottery was utilitarian, it displays a concern on the part of the potter with the production of well balanced, generally symmetrical profiles. These aspects can be seen to have dominated, along with the refinement of surface, until the Second Intermediate Period. Even, coloured surface coatings and overall lustre were features which marked the finer products, as did the use of light-coloured marl clays during the Middle Kingdom. This simplicity of style is reflected in the fine arts of the Old and Middle Kingdom and contrasts sharply with the elaboration evident in the New Kingdom.

A period of great affluence and generally higher standard of living, the New Kingdom saw a blossoming of the arts and the emergence of a taste for highly decorative objects. The concern with form and finish still occupied the potter but a wider range of more complex shapes was manufactured and painted decoration was in vogue. The same concern for balance and symmetry that affected the characteristics of the vessel profile emerges in the painted designs. The majority of the motifs were inspired by nature though they are not necessarily represented naturalistically. They were applied in carefully delineated bands or panels, and only in rare examples is there any sense of movement. The painter of the pottery was concerned to select motifs which were appropriate for the part of the vessel to be decorated, which were well balanced and which enhanced the characteristics of its profile.

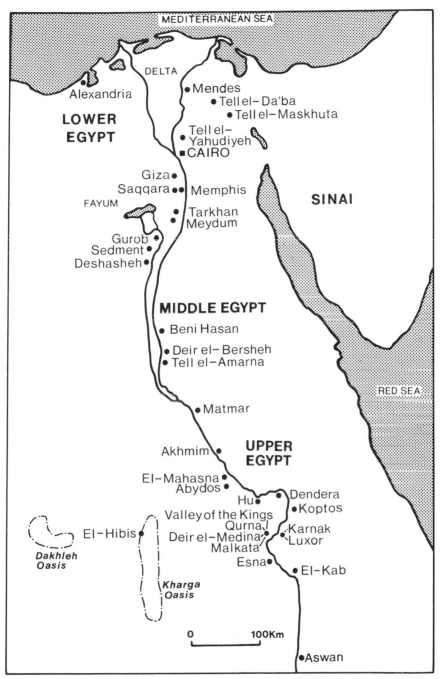

**72.** Map of Egypt showing the location of sites mentioned in the text.

The labels on the map are:

MEDITERRANEAN SEA

DELTA

• Mendes
• Tell el–Da'ba
• Tell el–Maskhuta

• Tell el–Yahudiyeh
■ CAIRO

LOWER EGYPT

• Alexandria

SINAI

Giza •
Saqqara • • Memphis

FAYUM

• Tarkhan
Meydum

Gurob •
Sedment •
Deshasheh •

MIDDLE EGYPT

• Beni Hasan

• Deir el–Bersheh
• Tell el–Amarna

• Matmar

RED SEA

UPPER EGYPT

Akhmim •

El–Mahasna •
Abydos •

Hu •
Dendera •
Koptos •

Valley of the Kings
Qurna •
Deir el–Medina •
Malkata
Karnak
Luxor •

El–Hibis •

Esna •
El–Kab •

*Dakhleh Oasis*

*Kharga Oasis*

0      100Km

• Aswan

# 7
# Select bibliography

Adams, B. *Sculptured Pottery from Koptos.* Aris and Phillips, 1987.

Arnold, Dorothea. 'Weiteres zur Keramik von el-Tarif', *Mitteilungen des Deutschen Archäologischen Instituts Abteilung Kairo,* volume 28 (1972), 33-46.

Arnold, Dorothea. 'Wandbild und Scherbenfund', *Mitteilungen des Deutschen Archäologischen Instituts Abteilung Kairo,* volume 32 (1976), 1-34.

Arnold, Dorothea. 'Gefässe, Gefässformen, Gefässdekor', *Lexikon der Ägyptologie,* volume II (1977), 483-502.

Arnold, Dorothea. 'Keramik', *Lexikon der Ägyptologie,* volume III (1978), 392-409.

Arnold, Dorothea (editor). *Studien zur altägyptischen Keramik.* Philipp von Zabern, 1981. This volume contains articles in German, French and English.

Arnold, Dorothea. 'Töpferei, Töpferwekstatt, Töpferöfen, Töpferscheibe', *Lexikon der Ägyptologie,* volume IV (1985), 616-21.

Bachmann, H. G., Everts, H., and Hope, C. A. 'Cobalt-Blue Pigment on Eighteenth Dynasty Egyptian Pottery', *Mitteilungen des Deutschen Archäologischen Instituts Abteilung Kairo,* volume 36 (1980), 33-7.

Bourriau, J. *Umm el-Ga'ab: Pottery from the Nile Valley before the Arab Conquest.* Fitzwilliam Museum, Cambridge, 1981.

Brissaud, P. 'La Céramique Égyptienne du Règne d'Aménophis II à la Fin de l'Époque Ramesside', in *Hommages à Serge Sauneron,* Vercoutter, J. (editor), Institut Francais d'Archéologie Orientale du Caire (1979), 11-32.

Charvat, P. 'The Bes Jug', *Zeitschrift für Ägyptische Sprache,* volume 107 (1980), 46-52.

*Egypt's Golden Age: The Art of Living in the New Kingdom 1558-1085 BC.* Museum of Fine Arts, Boston, 1982.

Games, K. P. 'The Magnitude of the Archaeomagnetic Field in Egypt between 3000 and 0 BC', *Geophysical Journal of the Royal Astronomical Society,* volume 63 (1980), 45-56.

Guidotti, M.C. 'A proposito dei Vasi con Decorazione Hathorica', *Egitto e Vicino Oriente,* volume I (1978), 105-17.

Hayes, W. C. *The Scepter of Egypt. Parts I-II.* The Metropolitan Museum of Art, New York, 1953-9.

Holthoer, R. *New Kingdom Pharaonic Sites: The Pottery.* Scandinavian University Books, 1977. This book contains a description of the sources available in the study of Egyptian pottery manufacture.

Hope, C. A. 'Two Ancient Egyptian Potters' Wheels', *Journal of the Society for the Study of Egyptian Antiquities,* volume XI, number 3 (1981), 127-33.

Hope, C.A. 'Concerning Egyptian Potters' Wheels', *Journal of the Society for the Study of Egyptian Antiquities,* volume XII, number 1 (1982), 13-14.

*Introduction to Ancient Egyptian Pottery.* Philipp von Zabern (forthcoming).

Kaczmarczyk, A., and Hedges, R. E. M. *Ancient Egyptian Faience.* Aris and Phillips, 1983. This book contains some of the latest information concerning pigments.

Kelly, A. *The Pottery of Ancient Egypt.* Royal Ontario Museum, Toronto, 1976. This is a collection of drawings of Egyptian pottery.

Lesko, L. II. *King Tut's Wine Cellar.* BC Scribe Publications, 1977.

Lucas, A., and Harris, J. R. *Ancient Egyptian Materials and Industries.* Edward Arnold, fourth edition 1962.

*Meisterwerke Altägyptischer Keramik.* Höhr-Grenzhausen, Rastal-Haus, 1978.

Nagel, G. *La Céramique du Nouvel Empire à Deir el Médineh.* Institut Francais d'Archéologie Orientale du Caire, 1938.

Nordström, H-A. *Neolithic and A-Group Sites.* Scandinavian University Books, 1972. This book contains a detailed discussion of clay types.

Nordström, H-A. 'Classification of the Wheel-made Wares', in Holthoer, R. *New Kingdom Pharaonic Sites: The Pottery,* 60-7.

Nordström, H-A. 'Ton', *Lexikon der Ägyptologie,* volume IV (1985), 629-34.

# 8
# Museums to visit

The museums listed here are known to contain Egyptian pottery, although this is not a comprehensive list. Intending visitors are advised to find out the times of opening before making a special journey.

## Great Britain

*Ashmolean Museum of Art and Archaeology,* Beaumont Street, Oxford OX1 2PH. Telephone: Oxford (0865) 512651.

*Bolton Museum and Art Gallery,* Le Mans Crescent, Bolton, Lancashire BL1 1SA. Telephone: Bolton (0204) 22311 extension 379.

*British Museum,* Great Russell Street, London WC1B 3DG. Telephone: 01-636 1555 or 1558.

*City of Bristol Museum and Art Gallery,* Queens Road, Bristol, Avon BS8 1RL. Telephone: Bristol (0272) 299771.

*Durham University Oriental Museum,* Elvet Hill, Durham DH1 3TH. Telephone: Durham (0385) 66711.

*Fitzwilliam Museum,* Trumpington Street, Cambridge CB2 1RB. Telephone: Cambridge (0223) 69501.

*Glasgow Art Gallery and Museum,* Kelvingrove, Glasgow G3 8AG. Telephone: 041-334 1134.

*Hunterian Museum,* The University of Glasgow, Glasgow G12 8QQ. Telephone: 041-339 8855 extension 221.

*Manchester Museum,* The University of Manchester, Oxford Road, Manchester M13 9PL. Telephone: 061-273 3333.

*National Museums and Galleries on Merseyside,* William Brown Street, Liverpool L3 8EN. Telephone: 051-207 0001 or 5451.

*Petrie Museum of Egyptian Archaeology,* University College London, Gower Street, London WC1E 6BT. Telephone: 01-387 7050 extension 2884.

*Royal Museums of Scotland,* Chambers Street, Edinburgh EH1 1JF. Telephone: 031-225 7534.

*Swansea Museum* (University College of Swansea and Royal Institution of South Wales Museum), Victoria Road, Swansea, West Glamorgan SA1 1SN. Telephone: Swansea (0792) 53763.

## Australia

*Ancient History Teaching Collection,* Macquarie University, Sydney, New South Wales 2109.

*National Gallery of Victoria,* 180 St Kilda Road, Melbourne, Victoria 3004.

*Nicholson Museum,* University of Sydney, Sydney, New South Wales 2006.

*South Australian Museum,* North Terrace, Adelaide, South Australia 5001.

**Austria**

*Museum of the History of Art: Egyptian and Oriental Collection,* Burgring 5, 1010 Vienna 1.

**Belgium**

*Royal Museum of Art and History,* Avenue J. F. Kennedy, 1040 Brussels.

**Canada**

*Royal Ontario Museum,* 100 Queen's Park, Toronto, Ontario M5C 2C6.

**Denmark**

*New Carlsberg Gallery,* Dantes Plads, 1550 Copenhagen V.

**East Germany**

*Egyptian Museum,* Berlin State Museums, Bodestrasse 1-3, 102 Berlin.

**Egypt**

*Aswan Museum,* Aswan.

*Egyptian Museum,* Tahrir Square, Cairo.

*Luxor Museum,* Luxor.

**France**

*Guimet Museum,* 20 Boulevard des Belges, 69001 Lyon, Rhone.

*Museums of the Louvre,* Palais du Louvre, 75003 Paris.

*Sèvres National Museum of Ceramics,* Place de la Manufacture, 92310 Sèvres, Hauts-de-Seine.

**Holland**

*Allard Pierson Museum,* Archaeological Museum of the University of Amsterdam, Sarphatistraat 129-31, 1012 GC Amsterdam, Noord Holland.

*National Museum of Antiquities,* Rapenburg 28, 2311 EW Leiden, Zuid Holland.

62                                                    *Egyptian Pottery*

**Italy**
*Archaeological Museum,* Via Colonna 96, Florence.
*Egyptian Museum,* Palazzo dell'Accademia della Scienze, Via
  Accademia della Scienze 6, Turin.
*Egyptian Museum,* Vatican City, Rome.

**Sweden**
*Museum of Mediterranean and Near Eastern Antiquities,* Järn-
  torget 84, Stockholm.

**Switzerland**
*Museum of Art and History,* Rue Charles-Galland 2, Geneva.

**United States of America**
*Brooklyn Museum,* 188 Eastern Parkway, Brooklyn, New York,
  11238.
*Cleveland Museum of Art,* 11150 East Boulevard, Cleveland,
  Ohio 44106.
*Metropolitan Museum of Art,* 5th Avenue at 82nd Street, New
  York, NY 10028.
*Museum of Fine Arts,* Huntington Avenue, Boston, Mas-
  sachusetts 02115.
*Robert H. Lowie Museum of Anthropology,* 103 Kroeber Hall,
  University of California, Berkeley, California 94720.
*Smithsonian Institution,* 1000 Jefferson Drive, SW, Washington
  DC 20560.
*University of Chicago Oriental Institute Museum,* 1155 East 58th
  Street, Chicago, Illinois 60637.
*University Museum,* University of Pennsylvania, 33rd and Spruce
  Streets, Philadelphia, Pennsylvania 19104.
*Walters Art Gallery,* Charles and Centre Streets, Baltimore,
  Maryland 21201.

**USSR**
*A. S. Pushkin State Museum of Fine Arts,* Ul Volkhonka 12,
  Moscow.

**West Germany**
*Egyptian Museum,* Schlossstrasse 70, 1000 Berlin 19.
*Roemer-Pelizaeus Museum,* Am Steine 1, 3200 Hildesheim,
  Niedersachsen.
*State Collection of Egyptian Art,* Hofgartenstrasse, Residenz,
  8000 Munich, Bavaria.

# Index

*Page numbers in italic refer to illustrations*